Writing on Water

MOOJI

Writing on Water

Spontaneous Utterances,
Insights and Drawings

Edited by
Zenji and Manjusri

Mooji Media Publications

WRITING ON WATER

First corrected reprint 2015
First paperback edition published in 2011 by

Mooji Media Publications

an imprint of Mooji Media Limited,
PO Box 67093, SW2 9LF London, United Kingdom.

www.moojimedia.com | www.mooji.org

Also available as *special hardback edition*
from www.mooji.org/shop

Brush drawings by Mooji
Cover design by Jyoti Graziano

British Library Cataloguing in Publication Data.
A catalogue record for this book
is available from the British Library.

ISBN 978-1-908408-00-6

Dedicated to the
Mooji Sangha Team
Who serves with
body, mind and Heart
to share with the world
the Truth they have discovered
through Satsang

~ Mooji

Prostrations
at the feet of my Master,
the embodiment
of grace, wisdom and love;
the light of whose presence
dispels all doubts and delusion,
thus establishing the mind
in its original state
—unborn Awareness.

Sri Harilal Poonja

Beloved 'Papaji'

Bhagavan Sri Ramana Maharshi

The Sage of Arunachala

PREFACE

You hold in your hands a gem that could facilitate the direct experience of the mystery which is the foundation of the entire Universe. Here is an opportunity to know and become firmly established in that 'knowing'—which is that you have always been the timeless and infinitely perfect Being.

Many speak of the Truth; few know it directly and fewer still have the capacity to reveal it. Mooji is one of those rare beings gracing this planet who not only is awake, but is also able to drive the mind back into its source through the authority of his words and presence. In this way he demonstrates a unique ability to release sincere seekers from the dictatorship of the egoic mind.

Writing on Water is a condensed ray of that warm effulgence that is Mooji. Contained within are golden nuggets of wisdom gathered over the past decade from Mooji's notebooks, and from his private meetings and satsangs around the world. This book is also a treasure for its original artwork, which supports the written Truth. Mooji's brushwork carries no intention to capture any known objects. It is an outpouring of creative joy. His drawings express the spontaneity and freedom consistent with life. It is the belief in the mind's interpretations that limits and causes us to stray from the obvious Truth. One way out of this trap is to contemplate what Mooji shares and unswervingly points towards.

A broad-minded attitude is helpful in approaching this book. No matter what spiritual literature or teachings one has studied, living words of Truth will always be fresh and immediate. What follows is not offered for theoretical discussion or debate, or indeed to be taken blindly. Concepts in themselves are not fixed; they only appear that way when we confine ourselves to what feels familiar and move in an environment where assumptions are rarely challenged. Truth cannot be systemised into sanitised concepts, no concept being whole or original.

You are invited to dip your mind into this wellspring and allow your heart to fully imbibe the radiant wisdom gleaming from these pages.

The Editors

The whole point
of these sayings is to leave your
mind empty, not full.

If you go away with learning,
you have missed the opportunity.

Satsang is not
a teaching but a clarifying, so that
true understanding may be reinstated
and delusion dispelled.

I am not
a speaker nor a preacher.
I have no mission
to change the world. I have no original
words or teachings to give anyone.
I reflect only what I have experienced directly
inside my heart, in the most natural way.
I have no fascination for fresh ideas or activity.
All enthusiasm for worldly endeavours
and striving have all but gone.
For me, thoughts, words and deeds
—the activities of life—are merely the utensils
for serving out the
prasad of the Beingness.

the prophet
Mooji

Ultimately, it is freedom from
even the concept of freedom that we seek.
It is the end of striving.

We place our attention, our efforts,
into becoming the best 'someone' we can be.
That is the outcome of conditioning and
it is natural and unavoidable
till the truth is recognised and verified inside the heart.
Evolving towards perfection
is the whole story of humanity, but
it is not freedom, not truth.

By all means
live the highest expression you can. Change what you feel
is not in service to your freedom and truth.
Follow your heart's prompting but do not take
the expression to be the embodiment
or definition of the Self.

Enjoy, with gratitude, your life
as a gift from life itself;
as an expression of God; as the dance of the cosmos,
while remaining within as the formless seer.

The sage looks in the mirror of existence
at the image appearing as himself but he is not confused.
He remains the unalterable Being shining
inside the shrine of emptiness.

What hurts most is having to live as a 'me'
instead of pure 'I'-awareness.

❧

What is a good disciple?

A master in the making.

What is a master?

A successful disciple.

❧

Conceptual spirituality
has always been readily available.

What is rare, is Holiness
—that which shines by itself
when knowledge is swallowed
inside the heart.

❧

Beware! Experience emotions
but don't become an emotional accountant.

The ultimate trick of the ego-mind
is to slip behind the concept of the seer.
It then says,
'I'm not anything that appears.'
Only the wise will detect its presence
and root it out.

The Satguru's grace throws 'you'
out of yourself and enters your absence.

Your self-image is as ephemeral as the play of
light dancing on the surface of water.

As guests do not arrive at a restaurant
bringing their own menus,
do not come to life with your own
list of requirements.

Who will be content
with the meals that life prepares?

It is not
merely mind-watching;
but rather
recognising That
in which mind
is watched.

Realising no concept
has autonomy,
leave mind as open space.
Neither close any concept as fact
nor take ownership of it.
Most importantly, refrain from
identifying with any idea
however enticing.
Thus, you will not limit
your natural mind.

Self-inquiry
does not improve the 'I',
rather it exposes
the 'I' as mere thought,
and finally dissolves this 'I'-thought
into its source.

Who is saying,
I can't find the 'I Am'?

The 'I Am'
is speaking this in its
confusion as mind.

Even the label 'I Am'
is not needed;
you are the 'I Am' itself!

And you are That which the
words 'I Am' point to.

The world is full of mad people.
What is this madness?
Pursuing the trivial and transient whilst
overlooking the
Jewel of non-dual Bliss.

A thought may arise,
'It's okay now, but it is going
to be different when
I return to my daily life.'
Already you are
anticipating your downfall.
Recognise this as thought.
Feel its pull yet stay centred as
the uninvolved observer,
confirmed in the knowing:
this is untrue.

Although it is true
that practices by themselves
do not automatically
lead to enlightenment,
they do have an essential place.
Initially, they prepare
the mind to be receptive to subtle truths.
Once ultimate understanding occurs,
practice continues to assist
in establishing the attention
in the ground of Being
and to ward off doubt towards
what has been recognised
in the heart.

If you dip your finger in water,
it trembles a little;
when it is removed, the water
becomes quiet again.
This is the nature of water.
Similarly, the nature of Being
is such that if stirred,
It returns to its natural stillness by itself.
No help is needed.

But where there is the 'I-me' thought,
the finger
is always agitating the water.

Rather than
becoming involved
with the scene,
look for the seer.

❧

When a real meeting
happens between
oneself and the Guru,
both vanish.

Only the Satguru,
the indivisible Self, remains.

❧

One suffers not
so much
from the concrete world,
but from mental noise.

Inner space is
the natural resting place of all beings
—it is our place of true meditation,
stillness and love—
when hidden, due to false identification
with the ego,
chaos comes into the world.

There is no 'thing' beyond 'I Am'.
You, as 'nothing', are beyond 'I Am'.

Usually the questioner
is not questioned.
The questioner's question is
the focus of attention.
The majority of questions, being objective
in nature, can be satisfied
with objective answers in accordance
with our mental tradition.

However, as soon as,
'But who is the questioner?'
is asked, an earthquake enters the mind
and the false identity begins
to deconstruct, giving way to the light
of pure Being.

Truth,
though non-dual,
is not sterile.
No need to force one's life into
a flavourless existence.

❧

Many are they who
talk about
'God', 'Spirit' or 'Consciousness'...
Rare are those in whose presence
this Truth is evident.

❧

That which Is,
doesn't look like anything.
Mind looks like everything; every thing is mind.
Self resembles nothing.
No experience can be
the measuring stick for the Self.
So sublime, so beyond all imaginings
and the thinking mind is
the Absolute Reality—that which we truly are.

Realising this,
one moves from death into everlasting life.

Mind,
once swallowed by the Heart,
is burped up
as silence and peace.

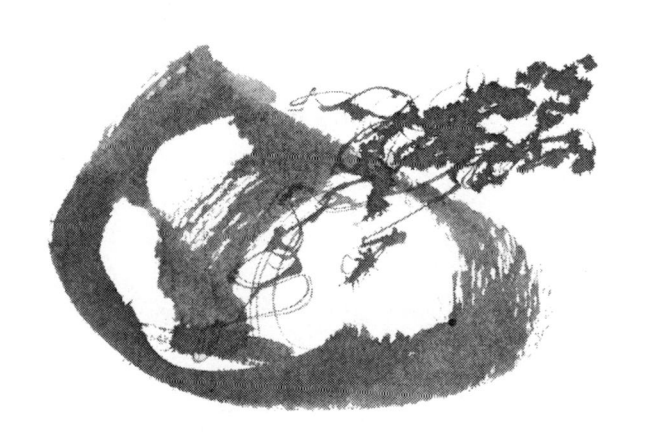

Death
is one of God's great ideas,
for the fear of extinction
drives the mind
to search for that which is undying—
one's unborn Being.

Mind will
always send you
on a journey.

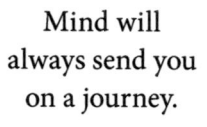

You are
total unicity
beyond duality.
That you are.

You are
so one with yourself
that you cannot
perceive yourself.
You can only imagine
that you are other
than that.

Like a knife that
can cut so many vegetables
but cannot cut itself,
or the scale which
can weigh so many objects
but cannot weigh itself,
so it is with the one supreme Self
—the sole Reality.

Being indivisible,
it cannot perceive itself,
it can only perceive
what it is not.

The highest sadhana is
when perceiving and being
are one.

❧

Be true to Love.
Do not betray Her.
Then, on the day
that the forest of the mind
bursts into flames,
you will not run.
You will remain silent and still;
for this is when Love bears
Her sweetest fruit:
untouched Presence.

❧

We are holding onto so much!
We carry around so many memories,
intentions and concepts
in the pocket of the mind.

Keep emptying your pockets.

Some rare beings,
seeing the futility of storing
the worthless,
simply rip out their pockets
and throw them away!

I am not giving,
finding or sharing Truth.
I am Truth itself.

＊

*Why do I feel so bound,
so unfree?*

Because you are trained
to believe it.

＊

The doctor says,
'You are going to die.'

This moment and message
you will not forget.

The sage declares,
'You are the Eternal.
That will never die.'

The next moment
you forget it.

How amazing is
the delusion that holds this
world spellbound!

*If the kiss of a lover
can set you on fire,
what will the kiss from God
do to you?*

*Allow yourself to be
truly kissed from within.*

*A kiss your mind
can never give.*

Eternity is not endless time,
eternity means timeless.

❧

It is you
who determine
whether something
happens or not.

It is an option,
an appearance, not a fact.
Without interest
there is no registration
—nothing 'happens'.

If you believe in and
identify with a movement
—there is a 'happening'.
Right there it begins writing
itself into your memory.

Such is the nature
and mechanism of the mind.
Therefore, abide as
Awareness only.

❧

The ways of the mind are ancient
but your Self is timeless.

God
offers you bread.
Don't ask for toast,
make it!

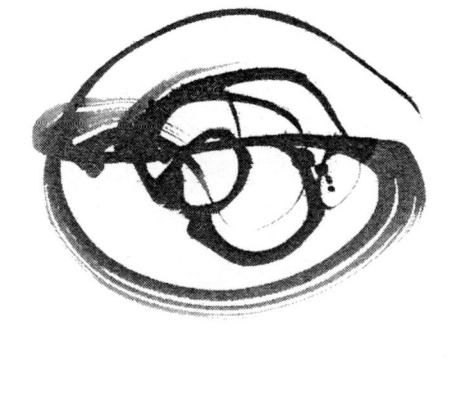

What is it
that cannot be altered or removed?
How much distance stands
between yourself
and that which cannot
be taken away?

Only the distance of a thought.

As knowingness is known,
the very knower vanishes.

But even 'vanishing' is an illusion.
The immutable Self is transcendent to all,
beyond appearing and disappearing.

Ineffable!

Through trust in the master's words,
the cataract of mistaken identity
is peeled away,
revealing the indivisible Self.

And so falls away the weight
of ego-centred conditioning, arrogance,
pride, fear and all suffering.

One comes to see—not the Self—
but purely from the Self,
the transience of the phenomenal world.

Cease trying
to explain the mind.
Simply be the Self.

❧

Words pointing from
Truth to Truth
return to Emptiness
once their mission
is complete.
Therefore, they are not to be
collected and displayed
in the museum of the mind.
By turning living words into rigid concepts,
they become a sarcophagus
for the aspirant.

❧

Why do you require so much
before you will allow
yourself to simply rest as Being.

Discard this checklist
for enlightenment. It is only
the mind's concoction to cheat you out
of the peace you already are.

Nothing is
greater than everything.
All 'things' sprout out
of no-thing and
finally dissolve into
nothingness.

Nothing Is.

❧

The one who walks
without desire, expectation
or identity,
is called the Buddha.

❧

Having looked and
understood the correct position
of the Self with respect to projections,
now keep your attention
inside the Self.
Like this, everything
becomes quiet.
The mind actually loves being here;
it just fights initially,
because it is accustomed to being
outside in the playground
called existence.

Knowing all is mind
and that there is
nothing to attain to be 'oneSelf',
Ananda shines in the heart.

If you seek
forgiveness of God
for offending your neighbour,
ask forgiveness
from your neighbour
and you will receive it from God,
who is the innermost Being
of both yourself and
your neighbour.

You are free!
But you must determine
as *what* are you free.

You want to be
free as the ego.

But you have to be
free *of* the ego.

—

Thoughts will arise.
This in itself does not constitute thinking.
It is only when the thought 'I'
engages with them
that psychological thinking and
the thinker are born.

—

Relationships
become claustrophobic
if they keep you
in a state of personal identification.

When they serve to reflect
your universality,
they are a mirror, a tool of liberation.

My love,
leave aside all this
fruitless thinking
and come
lay down here,
in the silence of Being.

Tasting the seasons of life
without adding
the seasonings of a deluded mind
—what freedom!

❧

You can never be lost.
What can be lost
is your way of thinking about yourself,
your identity with limitation.
It is the conditioned mind that says, 'I'm lost.'
Let mind be lost.
Lose your mind. Lose your mind
inside your heart.

❧

The liberated one has
transcended the programmed life
for he has realised
the illusoriness of the world.
Knowing the world is nothing but
the gross form of the mind,
he remains in effortless Self-awareness
unconcerned with the outcome of life's play.
His actions, though detached,
are always full of grace, compassion and wisdom.

The ego cannot smell its own breath.

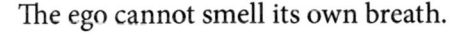

The point is:
You need only say 'yes'.

Say 'yes' to Truth.
Say 'yes' to Freedom.
Say 'yes' to whatever it takes
to be fully free from
the grip of the egoic mind.

Make no compromises,
no deals, no bargains.
No contract is required.
Just say inside your heart,
'I am open, take me.'

That itself is a mighty prayer,
a true surrendering
which can never be refused.

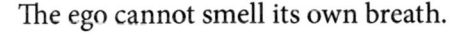

Pure mind is empty mind.
Once the curtains of the mind are pulled apart,
nothing is found there except a mirror,
and this mirror reveals:
What you are seeking is your own being.

Baptise
your mind in the
heart of Being
over and over again.

If you think you are a person
—forget yourself.

If you think you are the Being
—remember yourself.

When you know you are Awareness
—there is nothing to remember
or forget.

In the search for the Ultimate,
learning alone has proved inadequate
time and time again.

Only by merging the mind inside
a heart of pure understanding
will knowledge become knowingness,
and finally transmute
into intuitive experience.

Some
are attached to
concepts and others are
attached to the
concept of non-concept.
Both have missed
the Truth.

I know
every human being.
Beingness in all its expressions,
I know intimately.
I see my own Being
reflected in their eyes.

This power you also have.

Self is not meeting another,
it is meeting itself
appearing as 'other'.

You love this life?

Great! It is the ultimate software,
a divine program. The password is: 'I'.

If you know what the true 'I' is,
then you can master this infinite game.
Without this knowledge, you as
the 'I'dea, enmeshed in the program,
continue an illusory evolution,
unaware of your transcendental state.

As the programmed 'I', it appears you can
do anything: create, evolve, interact,
meditate, explore countless dimensions,
still, you will not escape the game.

To be free, you must recognise
the player, the phenomenal 'I', is itself
an object of perception within you.

You are the witness.

Recall this!

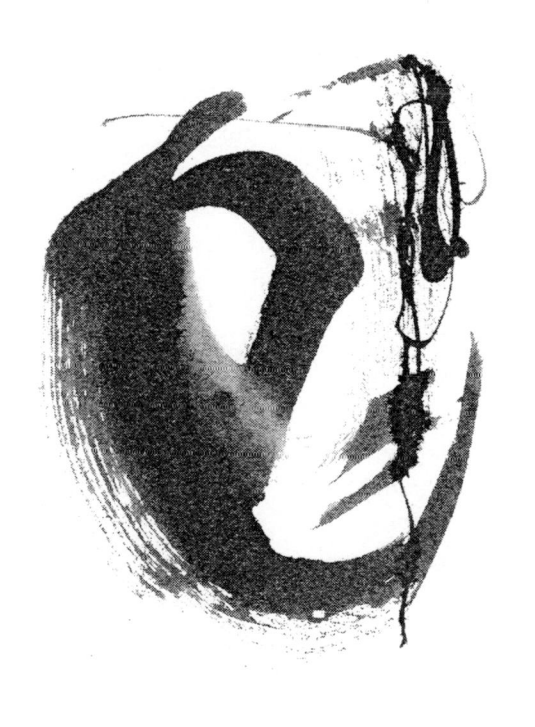

Mind will never be pure
as long as it carries the smell of a person.
Personal identity is the very pollution of mind.
When the person is recognised as
merely a mask worn by the Formless,
the mind remains
identical with its Origin.

Actions happen
but where is the doer of them?

Knowing, in the belly of my heart,
I am nothing other
than the immutable Self,
vast as the open sky
and boundless as space,
there is no such action as transcending
thought.

Remain consciously in the height
of your unassociated Being.
Like this, your mind becomes sanctified,
showering blessings upon the world.

The secret of the Buddhas
is that, unlike the regular man,
they see their lives
as nothing.
Knowing everything begins and ends
in zero, they have nothing to gain or lose
from this world.

Unfathomable is the joy of the liberated.

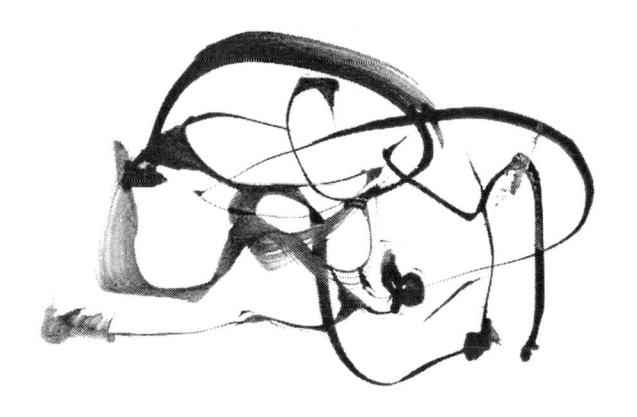

Go beyond all modifications of mind,
including the intimate sense
'I Am'.
Be entirely empty. Be effortless.
When peace and joy appear,
welcome their presence,
for they have come not only
as the perfume of the Self, but also to sweep
the house of Being.
It must be clear to you that they are arising
in the space of your Awareness-Self.
Be one as that Awareness only.
This is the essence!

Having forgotten
everything,
one effortlessly remembers

Nothing!

In the same way
that your fingernail can
cover the sun,
a concept believed in,
can eclipse the intuitive recognition
of the Infinite.

Upon realising the Self,
which is also known as awakening,
enlightenment or liberation,
one does not automatically become a teacher.
Becoming a teacher is not a natural
progression of Self-realisation.
Teaching does not imply the highest expression
of the Self. Like trees freely supply
life-giving oxygen unthanked, the realisation of the sage
need not be announced or recognised
in the world.

Judging others,
criticising the world;
one curses
one's own reflection.

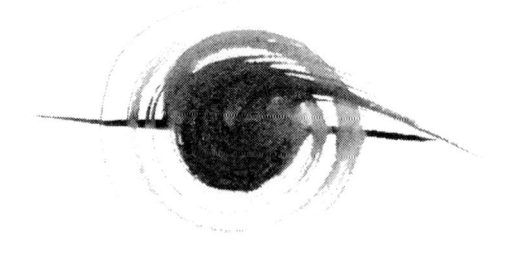

Love,
exploring and experiencing itself,
is what we are in expression.

Earlier,
yet imminent in manifestation,
we are the infinite
and indivisible One.

There,
beyond even the
immaculate conception:
'I Am'.

Look!
I'm not inviting you to learn,
but to actually recognise
your true position
through seeing, here, now, directly.

Otherwise, you may leave here
with what you call a better understanding,
but it will not last.

There is no one there to understand,
there is just understanding,
which flourishes in you as peace, joy and
contentment.

You are already
what you seek, but you must
know this completely.
It has to be recognised consciously
and permanently with mind,
heart and inside every cell of your being.

Don't postpone
this rare opportunity, otherwise,
you will remain asleep
and this sleep is a death and a dying.

What is to be awake?
Knowing that which sleeps and That in whose
presence the sleeper is seen.

Hold back a little from the usual reactions,
and allow the intuitive power
more room to be felt and expressed.
This is true self-control.

If indeed you have come
here for Truth,
then, whatever you hear from me
must strike you in the heart.

If it resonates with you,
it will evoke some inner response.
If not, the spirit of my words
will not stay with you.

Like an examination
you study merely to pass,
it will pass by you.

We judge others
by our own inconsistent standards.
How would it be if we could view their actions
from their own standpoint?

Would there not be empathy,
understanding, appreciation and even love?

When you
transcend the finite,
others feel their
own spaciousness reflected
through you.

Endeavouring
to overcome conditioning,
we can inadvertently pick up
new conditioning
in the form of spiritual identity
and its practices,
thereby missing altogether
the primordial and ever present
contentment
natural to our Being.

The one
who complains about
the world is revealing his
own entrapment
in the world.

An attitude of gratitude
is beatitude.

Do not make
the mistake of regarding those
who criticise others
as being on a higher plane
of understanding, for they,
by this very display, demonstrate
lingering attachments
to duality and ignorance of the
omnipresent Truth.

You cannot
discover Truth by studying
books alone;
you must dive inside
your own Being and find the pearl
of non-conceptual
Wisdom.

Consciousness,
in its highest aspect,
does not serve
self-empowerment
but rather dispels delusion.

If someone
criticises
another in your presence,
make sure you do not imbibe their
view inside your heart and
then judge the accused by an
inherited opinion.

I want to tell you this:
Right there in the midst
of the biggest crisis,
the most overpowering fear,
lies a portal to the Infinite.

It is immovable, sacred
and open to those who have
the courage or the desperateness
to surrender all for Truth.

The idea
you have of yourself
is struggling with other ideas
it has of itself.

The one who
begins the inquiry
will not
finish the inquiry,
but will be
finished by the inquiry.

There is a stillness in you
no heavenly or earthly being
can remove.

In front of it,
the mind is performing
and somehow
attention goes there.

Behind
is pure Silence
—your real Being.

All this is your dynamic dance.
As you stay rooted in
impersonal seeing,
the inner and outer are
revealed as One.

Knowing this,
you will not
suffer existence.

Let the mind be there
but don't 'have' a mind.

There comes a time when
man becomes tired of himself.

It is not the mind which says,
'I am tired', it is the Beingness which
becomes tired of the mind.

Only then will the real search
for Truth awaken.

As long as there remains
a desire for experience,
the search for Truth is delayed.

The seeker's mind divides
and the opportunity to merge
with the Heart is missed.

Know this seeker
to be the mind
in its aspect as attention.

Blessed is
the one
whose life
is the evidence
of Truth.

When Grace has
picked you up,
nothing can
overpower you.

Quite often,
the Consciousness
hangs out in a familiar
and lowly state.

Its tendency is to revisit
the red light district
of personal thought.

As you become aware
of this habit, a natural
disassociating ensues.

Keep the attention
in neutrality.

None can deceive, flatter
nor impress God.

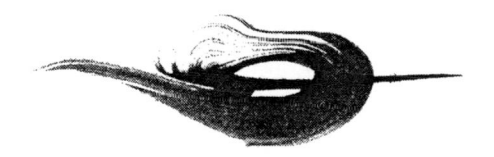

The master gives you
insight and courage to cut
the umbilical cord
to delusion.

You hesitate,
imagining it too high
a price to pay.
Therefore, you remain under
a spell, still loyal to
your identity.

Although you may feel
that you are on the road to Freedom,
there is an avoidance
to reach the destination, for
you are still living with denial and fear
inside your heart.

Perfection
is shy to show
her beauty.
She reveals it only inside
a mind made serene
through parting company
with the ego.

Once
the spell of delusion is broken
through inquiry, keep that
inner space empty by remaining
without identity or self-image.

Be one as Oneness.

For a while, the old tendencies,
though unreal, will attempt to force
their way back into position
to recapture freshly conquered ground.
Momentary and fleeting impressions will
take on a greater proportion;
but you are to hold your ground
as the undivided Seer.

All struggles end.

Know there is neither
beginning nor end for the Self.

When you think you
know something,
pride, opinions and argumentativeness
can be your emission.

When you know you
know nothing,
an air of openness and humility
pervades.

Then real understanding
enters the mind.

Whoever
hears my words and recognises
within the heart that
which they point to and from,
this one is free in this life.

If you want to see
yourself, you look in the mirror.
If you want something
other than yourself, you don't look
in the mirror,
you look in a shop window.

Awakening
is not for 'me',
it is awakening of
universal Consciousness
within form.

Love and truth
are not food
for my soul, for I am
ever complete
and content in my wholeness.

Wisdom and love
are the emanations of my abiding
Reality.

Keep sitting
in the chair of your own Being;
don't get up and move
about in pursuit
of mind's projections.

Wash your hands
of the sense of doership and
remain as effortless joy.

Mind is really a friend
who helps test and sharpen
your Dharma eye . . .

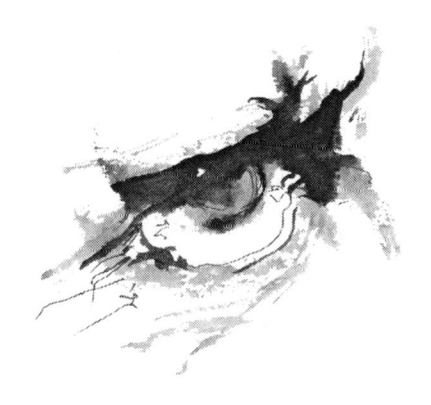

but
if you identify
yourself as a person
instead of Consciousness,
mind can often appear as your enemy.

May your self-consciousness
be absorbed in Self-consciousness.

In the psychic
climate of the
body-mind existence,
the Supreme Being governs
in accordance
with Its inscrutable will.
There is no 'other' to influence
the will of the Supreme.
Even the sense of a 'someone'
surrendering to the unfolding play
of existence is itself
the will, grace and action
of the Supreme.

If your heart's contentment
is dependent upon another, it won't last,
for 'other' will always change.

A genuine teacher
does not encourage clinging
but guides the student
into recognition and awareness
of the Indivisible.

People bear
their own 'suffering' better
than you suffering
on their behalf.

You have been
an apprentice long enough;
it is now time
to shed your protective skin.

Trust!
And stand upon your insight,
with understanding and conviction
gained through your own satsang.

Be courageous!
Do not be afraid to walk alone.
Be bold in your stance as Truth.

Just as you wash
your hands before eating,
clear your mind before
engaging with the world.

The ego has
self-interest, particular interest,
qualitative interest
in what is being perceived.
When this is recognised, a deeper seeing
becomes evident, which is not personal.
That witnessing power
houses the personal seer, and
recognises that the personal seer itself
is an apparition.

Experiencing
is pure,
when the experiencer
is the Self.

⁙

Satsang
scoops you out.

It scoops out
the mental cholesterol from
the artery of the Being,
allowing existence
to flow from
the Heart of freedom.

⁙

The 'I Am' itself is
the earliest extension,
and this is missed.

'I Am' extends out of the
unfathomable Awareness-Being.

In the realm of knowing and perception,
the 'I Am' is the earliest,
purest reflection of the Absolute
as material existence and cognitive reality.

Beloved,

Grace is divine love that flows undeserved.
We are never separate from Grace.
However, blindfolded by ignorance,
we remain unaware of Its infinite presence.

There is abundant Grace, yet we are
like fishes dying of thirst in the ocean.
We are the embodiment of Grace.
If we could bottle It, It would be the most
desired, yet desire cannot capture Grace.

Grace does not serve the ego,
but It strengthens us to be free
from ego's influence.

Every being is touched and supported
by Grace. Attempting to catch Grace,
It becomes illusive.

Honour and love Grace, and
It becomes your own.

The grace and presence
of the Satguru
is the vessel that carries you across
the stormy seas of delusion,
to the safe shore
of awakened Being.

In the highest sense,
it returns your mind, not you,
to its natural abode,
the Heart of the Universe.

Don't speak
merely because it is possible.
Speak only
because your heart is compelled
to express what is true.

᯼

Just for a moment
remain without association:

Leave everything aside
in order to recognise
who you are when
you don't turn to what's next.

᯼

With the arising of 'I',
personal identity quickly sprouts.

The seeker of Truth
must inspect
the 'I' sense, observing what costume
it wears in each moment.

Like this,
its chameleon nature being exposed,
'I' returns to rest as
unalterable Awareness.

Think of yourself, and
a subtle image is formed inside the mind.
You are not this,
nor any image or thought.

You are the silent
and formless Awareness,
within which innumerable impressions
appear and disappear
without trace.

Why say, 'I will never...'?
You are not the doer of action.
The life force is.

Your self-definitions
are constantly being exposed
as limitations,
so you may outgrow them.

Without self-definition,
one remains
as immeasurable as the heavens.

﷼

Our true love
is not for the body,
it is for sentience,
the intelligent source
of all life.

The value of all existence
arises from sentience, which we must
come to recognise and respect as
our own Self.

Though sentience is unborn
and undying,
it nurtures its creative expression as
being and becoming,
and shines in them as pure Presence.

It is neither
good to talk too much,
nor listen too much.
Best to remain
quiet and neutral inside
your own Being.

The mind is inert.
You believe, *not* the mind.
Your belief creates a world
on top of the world.

This great world appearing
in front of you,
and to which you feel you belong;
all of it, including
your sense of self, is as illusory
as the blueness of the sky.

Like a lengthy dream,
none of it is permanent.

Know yourself to be that
colourless sky.

The one who surrenders
everything, including himself,
and the one who finds
nothing, including himself,
discover the same Truth.

I want you to
find out, not what you
are looking at, but
where you
are looking from,
and with what identity
are you looking.

What you believe
becomes your experience.
As long as you remain identified
with the ego, you will both enjoy
and suffer your projections.
The wise, recognising
these tendencies, swiftly discard
them and remain as passive witnesses
to the tango of names and forms.

Goodness
cannot be found in the 'I-me' as such.

It is the *Godness* in the 'I-I'
that gives light to the world.

A true friend is not
merely someone you like
or who is like you—they could be quite
unlike you in most respects—
but one whose allegiance is firstly
to Truth, not to you . . . such a friend
is rare indeed!

If one has no faith in anything
at all, including oneself,
one must either be completely lost
or completely free.

It does not matter what
your mind thinks.
All thoughts are tourists.
Make use of them, but do not offer
tenancy to any concept.
Don't be a landlord of a mind-field.

All of us
are here before time began.
Have no doubt.
You are the witness of time,
not the victim of time.

The body is a burning candle!
You must know yourself
beyond this time-body while the flame
of Consciousness burns in it.

You are the pure Being, not for the time being!

Hold the attention in presence
and all else will be absence.

We have been conditioned
to believe that we are
the thinker of thought and
the doer of action.

If the thinker-doer is
understood to be
a sense and not a fact
—suffering cannot prevail!

Who are you
whose name is
'I Am'?

🥀

Insight untangles
the complexities of personal mind
and redirects its attention
to unborn Awareness.

🥀

Beware
of the posture or pretence
of 'helping' others.

It may be nothing more
than a masked avoidance
in facing one's own misconceptions
born of a deluded mind.

By holding onto one's indivisible Being,
all delusions end.

The Self is revealed
in its non-dual compassion.

The ignorant strive to control life.
Life reveals itself to the wise.

As our true nature
becomes self-evident, mind loses
its rigidity, fear and exclusiveness,
becoming broader, flexible
and all-encompassing.
Here, mind and Self
are One.

❦

Meet your teacher
without getting into learning mode.
Just be present and open.
Like this, no separation will arise,
for the mind will retire into its natural state.

And here, take note: This natural state
is timeless and unbroken.

❦

Making trouble is a by-product
of being human.
It is an outcome of the identification
that Consciousness has formed
with limitation. And it is good that it happens,
because if it didn't, you might believe that
this limitation is your real state.

The one who is
truly free does not proclaim,
'I am free.'
That one claims nothing
and is 'no thing'.
But what mighty power
is that Nothing!

The potential
for picking up impressions is there,
and yet you can move through
this grand landscape completely at peace.
It is only when conditioning selects a movement,
engages and names this an event,
that the mind registers it in memory.
Otherwise, effectively, nothing happens!

The earth is ancient.
But your private world,
a projection of your psyche,
is birthed every moment
out of thought.

✵

Life
cannot be against you
for you are life itself.
Life can only seem to go against
the ego's projections,
which are rarely
in harmony with Truth.

✵

The mind cannot guide the Self.
It can only guide the sense of individuality
that wants to get somewhere.
The individual is restlessness personified,
a projection of Consciousness
in a confused state.
Itching to achieve, it is rarely content.
However, the Awareness you are
is ever unaffected and self-satisfied.

I can be
neither lost nor found,
for I am absolute
unchanging Awareness.

I grant myself the joy
of Self-discovery through
my instrument and servant,
the body-mind.

There is no 'other' than my
own self to find me.
I am the all-encompassing
Reality.

If 'I' is identified
as the body and personality,
then it will be the person's
responsibility to look after himself.

But if 'I' is identified
as Consciousness, then it
will be Consciousness' responsibility
to take care of the body and its affairs,
and It will do a far better job
than the 'person' can.

This is the joy and freedom
that the wise and surrendered enjoy.

Mind
is looking for a
master's degree.

Heart
is looking to the
master.

Do not
worry about
what 'others' may
do to 'you'.

Strive
only to know
yourself
completely.

Then,
you can move in
this world
like the wind.

Who
can
command
the
wind?

*Stop
managing
yourself.*

*Hand over
your existence
to Existence.*

*Keep on
dissolving like
ice in warm water.*

It is
the Absolute
which is
portraying itself
as the Consciousness 'I Am',
the world and the ego.

Taking yourself
to be a body, no wonder you
have all these ailments.

Taking yourself to be
the mind, no wonder you
have all these worries.

Knowing yourself to be
Consciousness, no wonder you
have all this peace.

Knowing yourself to be
formless, no wonder you
are the imperishable
Reality.

The mind
has got a gun to your head,
but only because
you think you have a head
to put a gun to.

᷍

What does it mean, 'letting go'?

It simply means saying 'yes'
inwardly to, and remaining as,
the undivided Truth.

᷍

Man may travel
to the moon and back,
but he cannot
travel to the sun and back.

Similarly, our attention
can travel throughout the realm
of the mind, but it cannot
travel to the Heart
and retain identity.

On entering the Heart's radiance,
all journeys end.

Only Heart prevails.

True
spiritual practice
is aimed at
seeing beyond practice,
into what is
effortless
and natural.

*I feel like God
is playing with me.*

God is not playing with you.
God is playing *as* you.

There is a Presence
which is more profound
than any thought.
It announces itself here,
in the heart.
It is ever present, stable and pure.
When the attention rests inside,
automatically the mental noise subsides
and Presence alone prevails.

This unending Love never abandons you!
It is you who abandon your Self
to hold onto what is passing and perishable.

Remembering 'oneSelf'
is to be firmly
established in the Heart.

Here, mind is only a shadow. Without belief,
mind does not exist.

'Do nothing!'
To offer this advice
you must
first *be* nothing.

❀

We are the Infinite Being
in its finite expression, the feeling
'I Am'—I exist. When 'I Am'
is recognised as identical with the Infinite,
all sorrows born of ignorance
come to an end. This is liberation
—the true purpose of life.

❀

Do not keep company
with those who habitually criticise others.

Especially, do not mix with those
who judge the manifold expressions of Truth.
Offer heartfelt guidance wherever and
whenever needed, based on the Truth you
have yourself experienced.

However, do not strive to convince
anyone of Truth.

You can live with many,
find the One
you cannot live without.

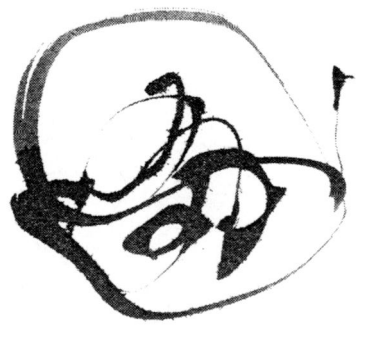

One of the obstacles
to the realisation of Truth,
is the belief
in the impossibility of it.

I want you to put this belief
to the test. Find out how and from
where this belief arose
by locating the 'believer'.

Real maturity is attained
when one's unbroken conviction is:
Nothing happens.

Like butterflies finding
the buddleia flower
without map or guide,
true devotees find the master
even if he goes
to the belly of the earth.

The state
of the awakened one cannot
be imagined, much less understood.

The mind cannot know it.
The intellect cannot analyse it.
Disciplines cannot attain it.

It remains ever unchanging
in its utter simplicity.

The one Self exists beyond knowledge,
being the source and illuminator of mind,
intellect and being.

You may say
the world is unreal,
but until the very unreality
of the one saying this
is confirmed
within your heart,
this utterance will remain
a shallow display.

Don't form
premature conclusions.
Let the clouds drift.
Don't try to control or arrange them.
Perfection shines in the eyes
that perceive
the all-encompassing sky alone.

Why
do you talk so much
about your feelings?
Feelings are ephemeral
—they are unreal.

Behind them
is a sort of feelingless feeling;
an impersonal space of
pure perceiving.

This is the presence
of the natural mind.
Beyond, lies
the Unspeakable.

Resting
in and as the Self
is not a task of
putting out fires.

Simply remain as
that substratum seeing:
empty of content or intention.
Don't strive for 'certainty'.
Who will be certain?

The Self is not busy. It does not
exert effort to get rid
of anything. It simply is.

I am like the size of an atom,
but this atom
contains the whole Universe.

When Awareness touches mind
—'I' begins.
When mind touches body
—'me' begins.
When 'me' touches object
—desire, attachment and
fear begin.

Together, the whole business
we call life!

Perhaps, 'death' could be
a more fitting title!

What I am pointing to
is not covered under layers and layers,
any more than the sun is hidden
from itself by layers of clouds.
The sun knows neither day nor night.

Know, similarly, what you are is
not altered by any condition.

Beingness
is not an achievement.

You need not do,
undo or change anything
in order to be.

The true Being is inscrutable
and beyond knowledge.

It cannot be found in the objective
or phenomenal sense,
for Beingness is the formless field
within which the very urge to seek arises.

You are already That.

There is no particular quality
to This that Is,
so don't join any concept with It.

The full grasping
of this ever present Truth
shines as joy, peace, compassion
and contentment,
and is called

Liberation.

The world is
not what you think it is.

The world is
exactly what you think it is.

If you keep indulging
the mind's play, you will miss
the untouched stillness
inside your own heart.

First,
start by only observing
without identifying.

See without interfering,
without wishing for change.

Even if there is a reaction
to what is perceived,
continue in detached seeing.

Like this,
life is recognised in its
higher aspect as an unfolding
rather than a 'making'.

The teacher already knows
you are the Buddha, but he won't
refer to you as that if
he intuits that your ego-mind will take
it personally.

Before the saying,
'The world is an illusion!'
is true, one's own delusion
must first be broken,
one's self-image
dethroned.

All cynicism and arrogance
thus dispelled, the manifest world
is seen in its true light
as the divine Body of Brahman.

Direct recognition of the Self:

'Direct' means One.
Whole. Complete.
Synonymous with Truth.

That which is direct
will not re-direct you elsewhere.

Self is home—Here Now—
beyond journey, distance and time.

Who is reading these words?
What comprehends them?

When the master says,
'There is no master or disciple,'
only those who are fit for
pure knowledge will understand
and appreciate the subtle implications
of a statement like this.

The arrogant mind,
fleetingly pleased by such an utterance,
fails to grasp the deeper
non-dual meaning until its
ignorance is dispelled.

The true Heart
cannot be broken or repaired.
It is ever perfect.
It pervades and encompasses
the whole universe.

Sometimes
Grace calls you to Emptiness
but you tie a rope around your waist
fastened to the apparent known,
so just in case emptiness feels threatening,
you can quickly pull yourself back
to the familiar.
Then you thank God for this rescue!

At the most
opportune moment of Self-discovery,
the mind will start shouting:

'Eureka! Eureka!'

It will plant
the flag but miss the seeing!

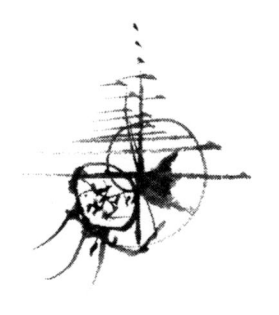

What is the measure
of an aspirant's progress
in terms of
authentic attainment?

They must evolve
to such maturity wherein
they are capable of bringing mental chaos
back to silence,
without requiring outer assistance.

The voice that says,
'I lost it!'
or 'How can I stay there?'
is the attention personified, not you.
Therefore, don't believe it!
Remain as Silence.

Ultimately,
the need to belong
is nothing more than the impulse
to dive within the
all-encompassing wholeness,
concealed inside one's
own heart.

This world
appears through the mind
to be divided into
separate beings of differing orientation
and type, but these are only
thought forms of Consciousness.
In reality, there is only
the One
Immutable Self.

What you are
did not move away
to make room
for what you are not.
The majesty of your Being
is infinite.
And the Infinite does not hide.

Strange, that the imagined
can conceal the Real.

❦

This root feeling
'I Am'—I exist—
was already present before a
name was given to you.

❦

Only by lighting the incense stick
will it release its full fragrance.

Similarly, only by lighting the mind
with real Self-knowledge
will it release its pristine nature
—serenity, joy, wisdom and love—
the perfume of the Self.

The one who sees
body, mind and world
as Consciousness,
transcends duality.

Having come to
the non-phenomenal recognition of the
Absolute ground of existence,
Consciousness has nothing more to offer.

What can be the reason for saying
such a thing?

Only form feeds on form,
but what is the food of the formless?
You are that formlessness!

When the personal doer is absent,
action and Grace are one.

You've always been!
However, you've been dreaming you need
to be something more, something else.

Imagining you need to be blessed,
to be healed, to be fixed, to grow and to attain.

Now, having seen it is just a play,
don't join anything further to yourself.

It was never true in the first place;
you only believed it was so!

Not one thing in the universe
has a single inherent meaning.

You do not
need to get rid of
the energetic presence
of fear in the body.
Just don't keep
the attention there.

Identify as the supreme
and all-inclusive Self,
the space in which
all phenomena appears.

It is this important
shift of attention, away
from the projection, towards
the formless Source that
exposes the fearful ghost of
ego as unreal.
Self alone remains as the
unmoving reality.

Start with your sense of existence
—the untaught way of knowing yourself.

Before you die,
find the Unborn.

Imagine
some high being appeared
to you with this offer:
I will give you the whole universe
in exchange for your Consciousness.
Would it be a good deal?

Beware of this feeling
that there's something to do!

Don't hold on to the sense of the person
who must do something
in order to be the impersonal.
Quickly detect this as a fraud
and throw it out.

Keep quiet.

Let the Truth be revealed out of your stillness
rather than groping for it.

Stop pushing.

Keep quiet.

It is impossible
to attain Liberation
whilst holding
onto identity.

When you live merely
as a strategist,
your life moves
like a river of sludge.

When you realise
your true Self,
life flows effortlessly
like a river of light.

You
continue to feel bound
because you keep
the ego in reserve and
hesitate to fully
trust the Self.

·❉·

You, Consciousness,
having developed
such affection for the infection,
'I am the body',
have seemingly fallen from Grace,
descending into
the realm of mortality.

·❉·

No need to set up
an immigration desk for thoughts
as the very immigration officer
is also a fraud!
Everything pivots around
where one puts the attention.
Focusing the attention
upon itself, the noise of 'otherness'
fades right there.

Happily knowing nothing,
one surpasses all knowledge.

Each one who has
offered up the mind in
satsang has been
shown the way to bring it
into silence and peace,
by remaining only
as the unattached witness.

First bring
the attention back to
its own source.
The outer and inner
worlds will follow.

You Are, even before
remembering and forgetting.

When you are free, all
who come into contact with you,
will be blessed.
Some may run away, but still they
will run away blessed.

Stay only as Awareness
in whose presence life glides by like
a play of shadows.

None of it is real.

This has been
so from the beginning.

Whatever comes, do not push away.
Whatever goes, do not grieve.

Like clouds floating by, all is perpetually
coming and going.

Again I say:
Stay only as that unmoving Awareness.

The Supreme is That in which
even space is perceived.
Therefore, You are subtler than space.

Contemplate this.

The one who is free
does not need will, because they are
one with the law of causation;
they are one with
the unfolding stream of life.

All of this is already
the Supreme Will.

But will you fathom it?

Upon reflection,
you admit,
'The one who is suffering cannot be found.'

Don't stop there!

Now, look for what is making this discovery!
Can that be found?

[*Silence*]

This inquiry will take you
completely Home
—beyond categories, relationship and time—
leaving you as you Are.
Then there will be no need to ask,
'How can I convert intellectual knowledge
into living Truth?'

For you will be this living Truth.

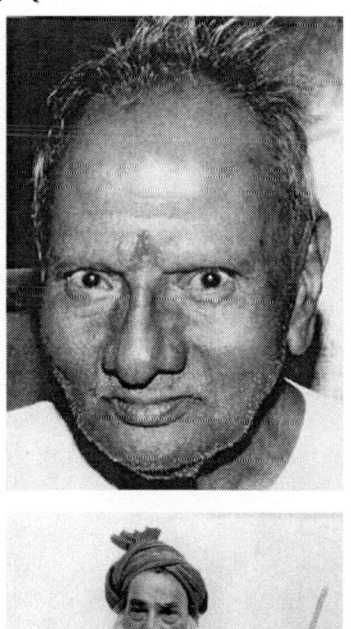

Revered sages with whom Mooji feels a close connection in the heart. *Clockwise from top left:* Sri Sai Baba of Shirdi, Sri Nisargadatta Maharaj, Sri Yogi Ramsuratkumar and Sri Ramakrishna Paramahamsa.

Mooji in Tiruvannamalai, at the foot of the holy mountain Arunachala.
From top left: receiving a fatherly hug (2011); riding along Pradakshina
Road (2008); prasad at Katu Shiva Pond (2010).

From top left: An intimate moment with little Shiva during satsang (2010); reading from the Avadhuta Gita (2010); Mooji's birthday celebration (2011).

Top: Mooji in Alentejo, Portugal (summer 2010). *Bottom:* meeting of the heart with Indian 'ammas' in Tiruvannamalai (2010).

Top: The sacred mountain Arunachala. *Bottom:* satsang at Vetri Rice Mill (2011).

These pages capture heart-filled moments of Mooji's darshan; a group photo at Sri Nanagaru's Ashram (2009); Mooji reading from the Ribhu Gita and with the editors at a special ceremony in India (2010).

We wish to save the world,
but it is ourselves that we
first must save. Because
only a 'saved' human
being walks with
integrity, gratitude
and in harmony
upon this sacred
earth.

If you simmer down the
best teachings on Truth, the residue is:
Be Awareness.

✤

Even to say,
'I must trust existence,'
is mind. The 'I' who must trust,
must itself, be mistrusted!
It is a riddle.
Find out for whom.

✤

Looking into the eyes
of others,
seeing beyond one's mental projections,
judgements and fears,
a presence is recognised that doesn't belong
to education, race or gender.

It cannot be described.
It cannot be defined.

Once confirmed
as our own Supreme Self,
we cannot fail
to recognise It in all.

Why do you keep saying,
'Who is to do this or that?'

You are not yet qualified to say this.
You are only parroting some
cleverness you have picked up
somewhere. Your presence
is still that of a person.

When I say,
'Keep the attention here inside the Self,'
you are to follow this advice until
the tendency for the attention
to go out falls away.

Ultimately, this advice will
also be seen as illusory,
both in effect and experience,
but for now the action

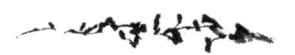

must be taken. Otherwise, the
natural state will not be
self-evident but merely felt as
an idea in the mind of the 'person'.

You will only be intellectually
convinced, and may easily believe
this conviction to be the full awakening.

This is a mistake.

To be awake means to be
effortlessly established in and as
the undifferentiated Self.

However, many are still attached
to their ego and merely imagine they
have transcended it.

Beware of this.

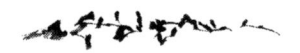

Something
has brought you here.
Something inside
is delighted to be reminded
it is nobody.

Mind cannot hide
the Self. Mind only draws
the attention away from the real.
Therefore, it is more true
to say mind distracts
rather than veils the Absolute.

You are only ever here.
Moving in 'hereness', can you
reach a point where 'here'
changes into 'there'?
Naturally, you are only ever here.
You can never be *there*.
Only with the aid of imagination
can you have the sense of leaving here.
Therefore, Here is where
and what you are.
Here beyond place and
Now beyond time.

The thought 'I' is the womb
of the phenomenal world.

I am the Self.
I am the life in my words,
and I am That
which they point to.

Even when the moment
comes for this body to fall,
my Being will remain.

Thereafter, Self-discovery
will become even greater for you,
as you will not be hindered
by any attachment you hold for
the form you call Mooji.

There is only one guru
and that is the formless Self, the
source of all existence.
Find Him within yourself.

Whenever I look at a thing,
I am never located in that place.
I am always at the source
of the very seeing.

Perception of all things
occurs to, and in, That
which is beyond all locations.

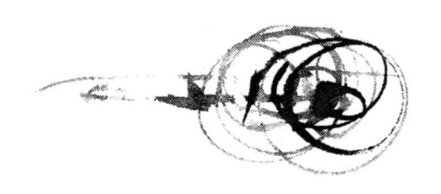

That which
you refer to as 'my mind'
is not stable, and you are making
your stand with it.
You have unwittingly chosen it as your beloved,
your guru and your own self.

It is the personal mind which resists
and betrays the Truth. When absorbed in the
Universal mind, it is no other than
the Supreme.

Awareness
does not need understanding.
It grants understanding
to the mind.

❧

Through the window of the mind,
see the world.

Through the mirror of introspection,
perceive the Unmanifest.

❧

Often, the ways of God appear
foolish to the ego.

But the ways of the ego
fall way short of the glory of God who
shines as pure 'I Am' inside the Heart.

❧

Mind is matter—Heart is spirit.
Mind is form—Heart is formless.
Mind is time—Heart is eternity.

Everything I tell you
is already known within you
as wordless intuition
and intimate being.

Can the seer be seen?

What is the point of this question?

To find out whether,
ultimately, you are material or immaterial
and to experience the answer directly
as your own
undeniable truth.

Self-inquiry
will reveal your original innocence,
your emptiness, your purity,
but it cannot reveal
your Self phenomenally.

Being the source of perception,
the Self is subtler.
In fact, it is beyond subtlety.

We
search
for
God

but
He is behind
the very seeker,
the seeking
and the sought
—unrecognised.

Who will catch this clue?

In most instances, a shift into non-dual
awareness occurs in the realm of duality
and doesn't last. It is not meant to.

Gradually, as duality is experienced
again, the mind tends to feel,
'I have lost it', while in truth, the primal
awareness remains the same as it
ever is—unchanging.

This insight must be confirmed again
and again, until it is one's irrefutable
experience, that the Self exists beyond
the play of mind and personality
and that we are that very Self.

Like this, the mind force gradually
subsides in strength and influence as
it gets pulled inside the Self.

This is a sober yet irreversible unveiling
of our original nature.

The potency of self-inquiry
is that you can look and examine for yourself,
not merely accepting what your parents
or anybody else told you.
You uncover the many cherished
assumptions held by you and are freed
from their influence.

The object and its perceiver
are both images on the screen
of Consciousness.
Is not Consciousness known?
Who discerns this Knower?

Sometimes,
Grace throws you and your 'world' into
the washing machine, full spin,
so that the fearful and controlling tendency
is compelled to offer itself
to the Totality—to the will and dance
of the Cosmos.

As your satsang deepens,
the debris starts floating to the surface
bringing much discomfort to
the body-mind. Now is
not the time for therapy or analysis.

Simply leave it to the
Sovereign Power whose benevolence
washes away all delusion.
Remember this!

Mind doesn't think.
Thoughts, being inert, don't and can't
believe in themselves.
It is the Self in expression
as the 'I Am'
that brings forth belief,
imbuing thoughts with apparent life.

Words
arising from Truth
do not require thinking about;
instead they draw
the sense of personhood
inside the Awareness-Self,
where divisions end.

Our natural state
is one of meditation without a meditator.
Words of Truth
cannot 'come alive' without
the presence of Being.

The sage is one
in whom mind and heart,
intellect and intuition
act in synchronicity.

Don't follow
your mind unless it lives
inside your Heart.

The ego mind
is kept alive by memory,
and the unquestioned belief
in one's self-image.

Thought is not something
to be afraid of.
It is something to be aware of,
but awareness is
without task.

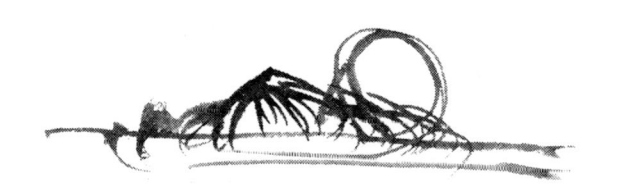

There are some beings who
in the search for Truth
forgot themselves entirely,
and today, centuries later,
millions of people all over the world
are unable to forget them.

Daily, new disciples
are seeking and finding Truth
in the names of Krishna,
Buddha and Christ.

It is not merely their body they seek.
It is the 'presence'—that deathless Being.

I tell you what is delightful:
To find an elderly person who is not
set in their ways.

❧

You are emptiness
appearing in the form of
a human being.

❧

God, Self, Consciousness
are One.

It manifests as different temperaments,
instilling faith, devotion
and love in some,
while an inquisitive, introverted,
or philosophical attitude predominates
in others.

God whispers,
'All are returning to Me.'

Given that each river merges with the ocean,
why hold the attitude
that yours is the sole or superior way?

All rivers lose their name when
they enter the Ocean—the womb of Being.

You have much
more to be thankful for than
to complain about.
But until you are fully aware of this,
you will continue exuding the noise of
discontentment.

Is it possible
to stop the noisy mind?

Yes, but not through force, for it thrives on force.
I will show you an easy way.

If you want to be a yogi,
you will have to practise your whole life,
but if you grasp what I am pointing to
with all your heart,
you will be free forever.

So what is the way?

Stop identifying with your mind's play.
Be the witness only, detached and impersonal.

Don't move from this.

Once you are stable
as the witness,
find out if this witness
can be found.

You are the
Unknowable
seeking security among
the apparent
known.

Thus, you acquired identity
and came into the field of duality
and suffering.

Awaken to your sleepless
Self!

Religion can guide you to Freedom.
But if not, beware
it doesn't keep you bound.

Honour your seeing.
Digest your seeing.

Otherwise, it becomes
just another thing you file away
in the mind's department
of philosophy.

You're here for much more
than knowledge.
You are here for Self-discovery!

O Lord!

Let my knowing of You
not just be in my mind but
fully alive
inside my heart.

Remove 'me'.
Let there be only You.

Love is
the transition from person
to presence.

Freedom is
observing the phenomenon
of presence.

❧

Your life is blessed.
But if you are still wearing the
old spectacles of identity,
attachments and desires, it can
appear full of strife.

❧

You are the Timeless
experiencing time,
because of this time-body.

In pure Awareness,
neither night nor day exist.
There is neither religion nor politics;
neither birth nor death.
No duality.
And yet, there is pure Love and Bliss.

What a mystery!

True knowledge and Being are one.
What we know
in the Heart need not be questioned,
it remains within as silence and peace.
All other forms of knowledge are merely
what we think we know.

Before understanding reveals itself,
misunderstanding
needs to be swept out of the way.
Understanding will not reveal itself while there
is investment in the unreal,
for that portion of energy will continue creating
distractions in order to avoid or delay
seeing what Is.

Such is the nature of the
egoic mind.

Insight is God's way of
Self-contemplation.

❧

Don't
allow concepts
to solidify or stagnate
by collecting them
as knowledge.

They are purely
momentary pointers to
the formless reality
experienced
inside the heart.

As soon as their
work is done
they return to
the emptiness from
which they spring.

They are the soap-bubble
mirrors of God.

❧

Don't read any experience
as a measure of yourself.
You are the Immeasurable.

I am your absence
and you are my presence.
You are my absence
and I am your presence.

And where these two meet,
a vanishing happens.
The Unborn is revealed.

That principle
that manifests as the master
is ever here now.
The true master never dies.
It is the 'mister' that dies.

The true master, that Satguru within,
alone is real.

Being here
is really just an invitation
to rest as Being.
There is nothing you need to do.
It isn't an invitation to become.
You won't be scrutinised,
nor will your actions be compared
with those of others.
That's unicorn food. Leave your self alone.
Simply observe and recognise
that all is unfolding spontaneously
when the inner journalist
—ego—is exposed as a myth.

Now that the mind
is clear again,
it is not that you have begun
experiencing peace,
but rather,
you are Peace experiencing.

❧

Talking about truth is not Truth.
Every lie is an aspect of the Truth.

Can both statements be appreciated?

❧

Don't fight with anything in creation.
Nothing is wrong with emotion,
only don't tie yourself to good or bad.
Don't cling.

There is no commandment:
'Thou shalt not feel.'
Feelings belong to the Totality,
like everything else in manifestation.
They have their place. Leave them there.
If you could embrace the entire universe,
it still would not add up to your Self. Nothing does.
Be very clear about this.

When I look at you I see only the Self.
I see the Self playing a game with itself
—a game called 'I want to be the Self'.

Be content only
with knowing who you are
and not knowing the rest.

If this is not possible
be at least clear about
what you are not.

How can one renounce duality
when the very renouncing
occurs in duality and therefore
implies separation?

The renouncer
can only be the mind.

Accept duality as the divine play
of Consciousness arising out
of non-dual unity,
witnessed within
and by the one Self.

Paradoxically,
Truth often brings the worst out of us.
It has to; that is its job.
After the worst passes,
silence and harmony prevail.

The world
does not owe you anything,
nor do you owe
the world anything,
yet it cannot exist
apart from you,
the Witness of the world.

❧

You give
far too much importance
to your mind
and none to your Self.

❧

Satsang means
to associate with Truth.

The result is the end
of association.
Something must go:

The one who associates!

This is a maturing.
Paradoxically, it takes time
to be established in the
Timeless.

This feeling
'I Am' is the Godly principle
announcing itself inside the body.
Without this 'I' nothing else Is.
It is synonymous
with Consciousness,
the seat of knowingness,
insight, peace and clarity.

It is the intuition:
'I Am without end.'

This is the one point that many
misunderstand:

If that longed-for realisation of the Self
comes in a thousand years
from now, the moment when it
occurs will be identical
with this moment here today.

Mind fantasises
about a lasting transformation,
but if and when that transformation occurs,
the One beyond transformation
will watch it.

That One itself is here now and cannot be
transformed.

Why do you
remember
the wrongs of others,
when you yourself would prefer
if everyone
would forget your own faults?

Inside the space
of pure mind anyone or anything
can visit, but there will be
no 'sleepovers'
for there are no guest rooms
in the infinity of Being.

Self-inquiry
is washing away all stale concepts.
All ideas of separation are
completely nullified in this seeing.
The previously unquestioned object–subject
relationship is completely transcended
—it loses its meaning.
When the fangs of a cobra are removed, its power
is gone. This is the potency of inquiry.

Mind can only
play 'hide and seek'
with you while
you are a seeker.

Everything
is pouring out of you.
When you know yourself as the Self,
it becomes spontaneously clear
that this world is arising in you.
All the beings, they are appearing in you.
You are in them, and they are in you.
It cannot be learnt;
it is a revelation.

When one discovers
the fullness of emptiness,
one wishes for
nothing more.

What is essential
is not only the master's power,
but the capacity of your
openness, your devotion.
In the meeting of these two,
Grace ignites.

Just see,
nothing is actually affecting you
when you just observe,
when you don't say, 'This should not be.'
Pay attention
to this wonderful power within you
that simply observes
without judgement, intention
or attachment.
Feel that space and peace.
Give it a chance.

The lover is chosen.
The Beloved is recognised.

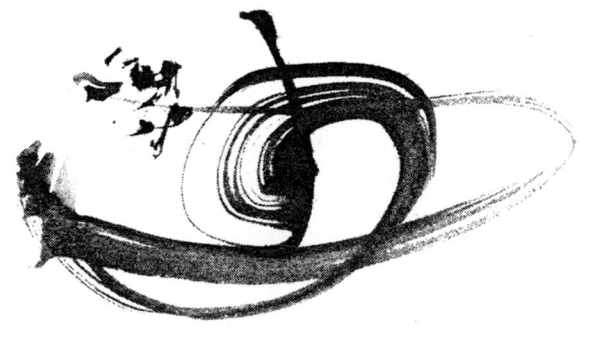

Feelings by themselves do
not create problems.
It is rather the tendency
to interpret them personally.

When out of habit
you believe the interpretations
that swirl up, it is there
that the bad smell of suffering begins.

Look a little closer at the lives
of all the masters. Prior to discovering
Truth, their minds were often in crisis.
A personal loss, broken dreams or
a rejection became the trigger to dive
deeply within and beyond the mundane
and familiar. An opportunity
for transcendence presented itself
in this way.

The same is happening with you
You are, through Grace,
compelled to be here in satsang,
because something within is unsettled.
A great doubt, an inner turbulence
or confusion is offering you the chance
to go beyond the personal
identity into the pure space of
impersonal Awareness.

The notion 'I am the body'
is the sleeping pill of the Being.
The belief 'I am a person'
turns the body into
the pyjamas of the Being.

Why strive
to be special
when you can simply
be 'yourSelf'?

Desire
springing from
the Infinite
entered innumerable forms,
and is experiencing
itself inside each form
as the intuition:
'I exist'.

All the 'I's
in their apparent
separate
expressions are all
lights flowing
from the single source light;
they are reflections
of the one
Illumination.

The seeker is not the Seer.
The seeker arises in the Seer's sight.
Can the Seer be seen, and if so, by whom?
Contemplate this.

Mind
in its highest aspect is
the Infinite.

I am
not here
to mystify
nor
demystify you.
My words are
only a mirror.
If there is an image
in that mirror,
reject it!

You are
neither the mirror
nor the reflection,
you are the imageless
Seer.

No God—No life.
Know God—Know life.

God is Truth and Love.

When you are
bound, the Beloved
comes in the form
of the master.
When you are
free, the Beloved
comes in the form
of the devotee.

Ego is a ghost terrified of dying.

There is a great
compassion in total
helplessness.
Stop trying to wriggle
out of it.
Surrender!

Then you will
see with serenity
that this is Grace
in disguise,
come to set
your mind

free.

Initially,
all thoughts are equal in weightlessness.
Your interest and attention
gives them weight and potency.
They have no other way
to derive energy.
Thoughts run on phantom power.

Can one walk away
from everything,
including the promiscuous 'I'?
How will it be done?
By recognising the impermanence
and unreality of all appearances,
including the 'I' itself
and staying as that which is 'I'-less.

The dreamer dreaming he is awake
remains inside the dream.
But the one who is aware of the dreaming
is on the verge of true awakening.
Finally, knowing the dream and its witness are
both dreamed images in Consciousness,
he recognises his invisible Self!

Holding your attention
inside the Heart of silence,
even the world
becomes the Unmanifest.

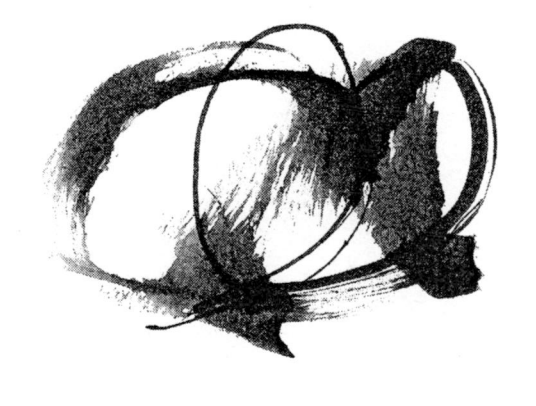

You have become skilled
at talking about the self you imagine you are.
There is no self that wears
all that stuff you carry. Be empty!
Keep some grasslands wild and open for the
workings of Grace to come to fruition.

Pain can be a great servant.
When present, other distractions
flee as one's focus is condensed into Now.
Don't fight.
Allow space for pain to be,
whilst remaining
as neutral Awareness.

With insightful training,
pain can become the torch bearer
to Transcendence.

When mind is left—Peace is left.

Imagining yourself to be
merely an individual,
you drift about in a world of
limitation.

However, when you know
yourself as Consciousness, you move
more like an environment.
Unexpectedly, help appears from
different directions, and so you come
to recognise the benevolent
harmony of the universe.

I am not a teacher.

A teacher has something to teach.
I have nothing to teach.

I am only pointing at what is being missed
while you look elsewhere for what is ever present.

I see needless suffering,
which paradoxically is needed
until the True is seen.

What is Real cannot be learnt.
It has only to be recognised in the Heart.

Grace
is not something that the master gives.
It is a benevolent force that shines spontaneously
out of his presence towards all beings.
However, it is most strongly felt in the heart
and mind of the
devotee.

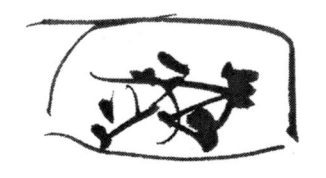

The restless mind
does not take easily to self-investigation and quickly
runs after familiar distractions.
In many cases, it must first be reined in or pacified
through the practice of japa, prayer, yoga or
association with wise and holy company.
Only then will it gradually develop the strength
and attraction to inquire into its root nature.
Gradually, this will result in the weakening
of the tendency to rush outward.
Eventually, the mind will sink inside the
Shiva Being.

Time and again,
your original eyes are returned to you.

Those eyes that see without desire,
intention and attachment,
see from the wisdom of the Self.

If there is an 'I' who can 'get it',
there will be an 'I' who can 'lose it',
and this 'I' is nothing but thought.

It is the most costly thought
when believed in, for it exchanges
your timelessness for decay.

Even maturing
is an illusion. It is inside
the mind and all that appears
in mind is mind itself.
Mind is the realm of illusions.
Who can say this?
The intellect of the Consciousness says this.
This knowledge occurs
inside and in front
of the unknown and unknowable.

There are many pathways
for the mind.
There are no paths for the Heart,
for the Heart is infinite
and pervades all.

Upon recognition of the
one Self, this discovery is made:

'All this, I am and am not.'

The world knows
and responds to this Love.

Eat the food
that life cooks and serves.
Chew with earnestness.
Swallow with gratitude.
Work with integrity.
Contemplate with devotion.
Sleep in contentment.
Arise in celebration.
Live in love.
Go your
own way in peace.

I put
a mirror in front of you
and you ask,
'How does it work?'

My love, carry on.
Yours is a great calling.
You are discharging
your river
of names and forms into
the nameless Ocean
of no return.
In doing so, others can
witness and taste, through you,
That which they have heard
only as rumour.

Mind is shopping for trouble
and you still appear to be up for business.

Closing the shop of self-interest
mind returns Home.

Could anything be perceived
were you not conscious?

Even God is appearing in your
Consciousness.

God can only appear
through and as
Consciousness itself.

God Is
Self, Consciousness
and beyond.

Insight and experience
may arise either from activity
or from inner stillness.
A sage attains great insight
and understanding, sitting quietly
inside himself.

If you keep copulating
with thoughts, you will produce
scores of illegitimate children.

You will be compelled
to look after each and every
one of them.

A full-time job relieved only by deep sleep.

Is time required at all to be yourself?
If something is placed in front
of a mirror, does the mirror need time
or effort to reflect?

The ego wishes
for pleasurable states
to continue endlessly but, thankfully,
nothing on the relative plane can
remain unchanging.
Just imagine laughing forever
—how monstrous an idea!
Pleasure and pain must alternate
to maintain the freshness and equilibrium
of manifestation.

If you cling to uncertainty,
the universe will
mimic and manifest
your doubts.

Your answers to my questions
are not for me but for your
own introspection, Self-recognition
and confirmation.

Only the ego is concerned with
giving the 'correct' answer.

Life has its own life.
It flows along its own course
in spite of the ever restless
projections of the ego.
The apparent autonomy of ego is,
unknown to itself, included inside
the cosmic current of existence,
for, in Truth, none can act independently
or contrary to the will of
the Supreme Being.

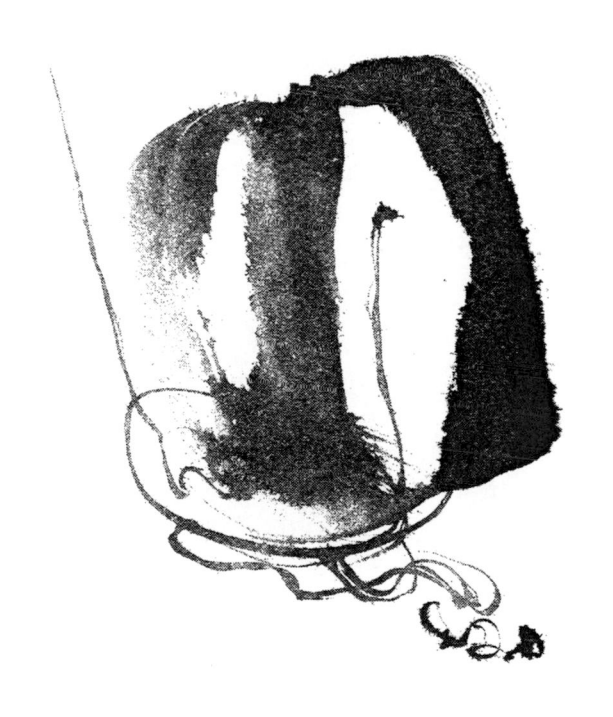

*Your ego
is so quick to interfere,
moulding life to suit
its projections.*

*Let life unfold
in silent equanimity.*

The Self
does not happen.
It is omnipresent and
eternal.
What 'happens' is
the recognition of the Self
by the mind.
This is called awakening.

Remaining as Awareness,
delusions fall away.
You don't have to sword-fight
any tendency. Follow this advice.
It works.

This unassociated
'I exist' feeling is pure.
Pure intelligence.
Pure intuition.
It is spirit.
Actually, it is a bridge between
matter and spirit.
But, Awareness is immutable
and beyond all.

I have no relatives.
I alone am. Absolutely.

Who says,
'When the search ended for me . . .'?

Is it the Self or something else?

When Truth blossoms
inside the heart, the person carries
the fragrance of that.
Truth cannot be unfelt, cannot be dry.
It is not a facade.
Ripe fruit has sweetness and fragrance.
A plastic apple and a real apple appear the same,
but there is no comparison.
One of them has no life.

You discern!

Searching
for love and personal
recognition
is the core vasana
of humanity.

Detached observing
is open
and trackless.
Leaving no footprints to follow,
experiencing remains
cool and fresh, light and free.

If attention
is allowed to wander aimlessly,
a state of fragmentation
and displacement
ensues and thus, the conscious
recognition of the Self
is missed.

Therefore, guard the attention
by keeping
it inside the Heart.

You ask for birth control
for your mind.
I offer the smelling salts
of self-inquiry to bring you out of
unconsciousness.
Take it.
It is all you need to recognise
your mindless Self.

You
are not here to fix the world.
Your opportunity
is to discover who you are,
and to know this beyond
conviction.

There is a mystery
bursting to reveal itself,
but it will only do so
inside a pure and worthy mind;
a mind free
of the bigotry of identity.

What I say to you
is food of the best kind,
but unless and until you chew it
well and swallow,
it won't get digested and assimilated,
and converted into living Being.

We mistakenly
feel that because a thing comes without effort,
it is natural and right.
We often use this as an excuse for our
actions or behaviour,
but the truth is
that activities around us
spring out of our psychic conditioning and emit
that corresponding odour.
The universe is not 'sending' anything to you;
action sprouts from the inside out and
is reflected as phenomena.
As identity with body and conditioning weakens,
the game changes in proportion
to the degree of inner spiritual maturity.

Why present postcards
of the body-mind and its imaginings
as a picture of the Real?
Recognise the one in whose presence
nothing stands apart, including the sense
of an autonomous self.

Satsang re-establishes the mind in its
primal state, the stateless state.

If you don't think thoughts are a problem,
then thoughts are not a problem.
That's a simple and easy thing I have found.

Sometimes
there comes a point
when your urge for freedom is greater than
all your fears put together,
it could be your greatest moment,
the moment when you leave your sense
of smallness behind.
The moment you release your Buddha-Nature
from the cupboard of the ego.

My questions serve only
as a trigger to push
your mind into the abyss
of impersonal seeing.

This is a mortal body,
but an immortal Being dwells in it.

Consciousness disguises itself as
the ego which has to awaken from
the ignorance of its real nature.

This is the challenge of Consciousness
playing as humanity. It must realise,
'I am the Eternal. This human form is my device
for contemplating my Self.'

Once you are clear
of your true position as the imageless perceiver,
you will find yourself again in the taste
of spontaneous existence.

You are the ever present Reality
playing as time, space, name, form and change;
fully happy in your unfathomable Being.

*When you live guided by
intuition rather than thought,
your life dances like
writing on water,
fresh and untraceable.*

Even if you
can't keep quiet,
keep quiet!

Drop the belief
that you need more time
and experience
to be
the Self,
for it is merely
another idea
arising in the eternally Perfect.

You know that you are here—you exist.

In order to negate or affirm anything,
you must already be prior to
whatever you will negate or affirm.
You cannot be what
you perceive,
for it changes right in front of your eyes.

You are not changing.
You are the unchanging Seer.

Rest as That.

How fortunate
is the one
who grasps this.

'Awareness of'
arises in non-dual
Awareness.

Unlike time, you are not passing!

While Consciousness
is available, that knowledge and taste
'I exist'
is present in it.
Make full use of it. Because,
only through the intuition
'I Am'
is the reflection of
the Absolute
felt.

Don't take yourself so seriously.

Ego cannot survive
without
the diet of delusion.

Am I a talisman or good luck charm
that people should come here
with their daily trials, or ask me to
bless their house or protect their
attachments? There is neither time nor
inclination for such things here.
Only those need come, who feel the
determination within that this must be
their last life and it is for freedom only.
They will not be distracted by the
usual concerns of humanity to the extent
that they lose the real focus, which
is to awaken to their eternal Self.
Those whose path is surrender
or Self-knowledge, and who will not be
satisfied with anything less;
they are welcomed here.

Don't
keep reporting these personal stories,
which are really
ghost stories.

You are not a ghost.

If you're going to be a ghost,
be the Holy Ghost!

When you have tasted
Nothing,
how can you be proud of
knowing anything?

꒞

Be still.
Day by day, become more and more intimate
with the inner stillness, joy and love,
which is the fragrance of your own pure heart.
Be still.

꒞

I don't know
if these words have any appeal for you.
If not today, another day,
another week, another month, another year
or perhaps another lifetime.

But at some point
—either through self-inquiry
or by surrendering yourself entirely
at the Feet of the Lord—
you will have to drop 'yourself',
that is, drop the idea of who you think you are.

From
the
highest
standpoint,
there is
no mind to kill,
no act to perform,
no pilgrimage to make,
no person to awaken,
no teaching to be followed,
no sadhana to complete,
only the unswerving recognition
that One Self is the unchanging awareness
within which all these are seen as
the dance of manifestation.

The operation
of Consciousness
has created the apparition
called 'me'.

❦

Fear breeds
mistrust and the need to control.
When you are controlling
you cannot be spontaneous,
you cannot dance;
you are too busy holding
your rifle to dance.

❦

Running after teachers,
reading, listening, meditating
—all were fine for a while,
but now you have the chance to see
that these pursuits took place
inside your own presence as Awareness itself.
You have been mistaking
your mind's projections as real,
when they have only been dreamed
inside your own Being.

This is what the sages discovered.

I Am the Body
is the universal bestseller.
All have bought it
except the very wise.

Be single-minded but not narrow-minded.

'Narrow-minded' is to focus
on the personal self,
the cause of delusion, deceit
and suffering.

'Single-minded'
means to be focused only
on the Universal Self.

How odd
that our first nature must
become second-nature.

The tendency
to judge others, to put them
down, especially in public,
is one of the sure signs of egotism
born of fear. The tendency
or reflex to find wrong in others,
to see where and when they fail
in our eyes is so we don't
feel threatened or challenged
by the truth their presence
highlights in us.
If only we would be as vigilant
at seeking out our own true nature,
we would be fully aware
and awake to the Real.

You ask me, 'Do you have bad days?'
You don't realise what you are saying.
How can I have good or bad days?
I am like the sky: empty, silent and boundless.
Can the sky have bad days?
Is it affected by the activity of clouds,
rain, lightning or thunder?
Like the sky, I am everlasting.

The Divine Mother
unceasingly embraces all beings
whether or not they are
aware of Her presence.
She is the indwelling Spirit.
Her cosmic name is
'I Am'.

You are already that
which you are seeking.
The real game of life
is to recognise this now
rather than then.

If
you looked behind and
beyond the thin veil
of mind into the Heart
of each person,
you would love them
completely.

Whatever your
differences, settle them
swiftly and lovingly.
Do not hold onto
a sore heart. Avoid
making anniversaries
out of your pain.
Offer no soil to
the seeds of delusion.
Make your peace with God.

Words
spoken and heard
in satsang,
point only to the wordless
and worldless.

Recognising mankind's will
is often driven by selfishness,
the wise submit theirs
to the will of the Supreme.

Finding the ways
and presence of God
to be in harmony with their
own inner Being,
they secure satisfaction
within.

Awareness
cannot be perceived.
Perceiving occurs in awareness.
You cannot
'look for', 'find' or 'see'
awareness,
for awareness is not an object,
nor has it any quality; it is non-phenomenal.
You, the seeker of awareness,
are also an object appearing in Consciousness
—the light of
indefinable Awareness.

❈

No intention = No tension.

❈

Experience, by nature, is changeful.
Feeling great today? Tomorrow will be different.
If you let mood be a measure of yourself,
your mind will be in turbulence most of the time.
Let all come and go.
It's not in the coming and going
that problems arise, but that
you attach such importance to them.
Therefore, they register in the mind as significant.
Simply, keep quiet.

If you want the
serpent mind
to live, then give it
the job of being
who you are.

Who employed you
to manage the world?

Mind is like food,
Heart like water.

Just as water is in food and
not food in water,
so Heart permeates mind,
but not vice versa.

Bring everything back to emptiness.
This is the leela of the sage.

Illusion in disguise
appears as true; when purchased
it becomes delusion.

I have no future,
therefore
I'm fully content
and supremely happy
as I am.

Reject knowledge
and be in knowingness only.
For whatever you think you know
becomes dead within you.

The Self is not delicate;
it doesn't need looking after,
it doesn't need healing
and it doesn't need prayer.
It is, without need.

This is pointing to what you already are
but have seemingly forgotten.

I have nothing to add to you, for you are
already complete in the eyes of the true Seer.

You must only confirm this
for yourself.

Without belief
a concept has no power.
With belief,
a concept can start a war.

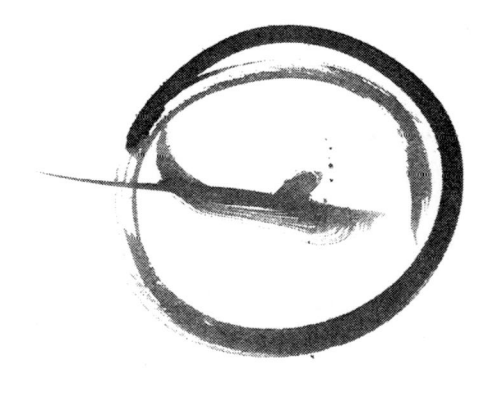

The statement
'I have realised the Self'
requires an 'I' who
has achieved something.
The Self is not an achiever. It can
neither lose nor gain anything.
It is eternally unchanging
and unalterable.

'Life sucks!'
'Who cares . . . it's all unreal anyway.'
Such thoughts are your
private terrorists.

❀

You are waiting for something.
—I am not.

Nothing can alter or benefit me.
I am beyond the play of opposites,
beyond even contentment
—I am.

I am non-dual Being.

❀

The highest teaching
is conveyed through silence.

But the seeker must be
ready to tune in.

Otherwise, silence is missed
and may even heighten
the noise in the unripe mind
of the seeker.

*In the light of real
understanding,
the unreal image of yourself
begins to fade, giving way
to a joyous sense of expansion
and spaciousness.*

'But I feel I'm dying ...'

*Though it feels like a dying,
you do not die. It is
the self-image that dies.*

I am
without beginning or end.
I am absolute Being.
I am the eternal beyond
the concept of 'eternity' and beyond
the concept of 'concept'.

Many fear death
but death only represents terror
to the ego and its projections,
for it is the ego that believes
it is the body and person.
For the one who has realised the Self,
death holds no terror, because
he knows he is the Self
and that the Self is imperishable.

What you are searching
for is already here, but you
postpone the discovery because
you prefer to enjoy it as
the fruit of your projections.

❦

The ignorant mind
is ever seeking
new lands to explore in search
of satisfaction,
picking up new burdens
along the way. Restless for change,
hungry for adventure, it misses
its one real refuge
—the Self
from which it springs.

❦

The question, 'Who am I?'
is the most compelling, most potent
at dispelling the hypnosis
of the mind. It is the smelling salts
put under the nose of the Beingness
which has forgotten its true nature.
It reawakens the Self to itself.

In the same way
that no one can share
your dream, no one can share
your waking world as
you perceive and experience it.
Both dream and waking worlds are
dreamed in
Consciousness.

❦

The world is in your mind
and your mind is in the world.

When the mind is in the Self,
the world becomes the body of the Self.

❦

Always at the point
of real atomic recognition,
the strongest doubt
and loudest noise will come.
Don't panic. They are phenomena.
You are the Witness of both
doubt and noise.
They happen *in* you, not *to* you.
You forever remain the
immaculate Self.

Let silence be your last word.

One day you will come
to see and find peace in confirming
that all this is nothing but
thoughts believed in.

A day not unlike today.

The state of identifying
with thought activity is called
monkey mind.

The state of
non-identification is called
monk's mind.

慢

If a thief enters a holy temple,
he will only notice the donation box.
Mind is the thief, the world is the temple.

Mind in the form of the ego
cannot perceive this holiness, because
it is blinded by its innate selfishness
and desire for the ephemeral.

慢

Even the greatest salesman
cannot sell you anything if you don't buy.
Like no one is interested in buying
second-hand underwear,
why are you interested in second-hand concepts;
those 'hand-me-down' concepts unquestioned
by your innate intelligence?

'I-me' absence,
radiant Presence.

⁂

Just as wind cannot crash
into space though it moves about
unimpeded, so does the mind
roam about in Awareness.

The wise know themselves
to be the Awareness
untouched by thought.

⁂

Experiment a little.

Take this attitude:
In any given situation, look
from the position or standpoint
of the personal 'I'
and observe the inner response.

Now switch:
Identify 'I' only as Consciousness
and feel the difference.

Choose the position you wish to be in.

Forget about yourself
—remember the Self.

❦

When I met Papaji,
there was that impact, I knew I was Home.

I felt his presence
in the room and inside my heart.
Even with eyes closed
the presence of the master is felt,
heard and seen.

The master
also speaks without words,
works without labour,
destroys without violence,
liberates without struggle.

❦

If there was no way out,
this world would be a dreadful place.
Thankfully, there is a way out.
And the way out is . . . the way in!
Dive inward. Dive Heartward
by inquiring,
"Who am I, who observes 'I Am'?"

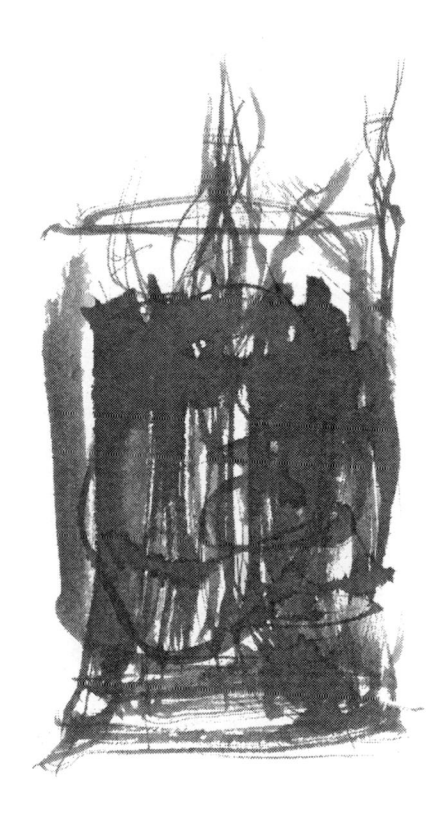

Repeatedly, you must
be delivered to the unsparing
inner fire of the Satguru;
the furnace that reduces
all arrogance to ashes.

Without self-deception,
life would be unbearable
for the egoic mind.

֍

You cannot go beyond life;
you are already beyond
as its witness.
Don't go beyond. Remain beyond.

֍

It is not
that you are too much in the world,
but more that you are not
enough in Self-contemplation.

֍

When knowledge
and experience unite,
superficial questions and doubts dissolve,
for they can only persist and prevail
while you have investment
in duality.

We are not equal
—we are One.
It is this Oneness
that is conversing with itself
in satsang.

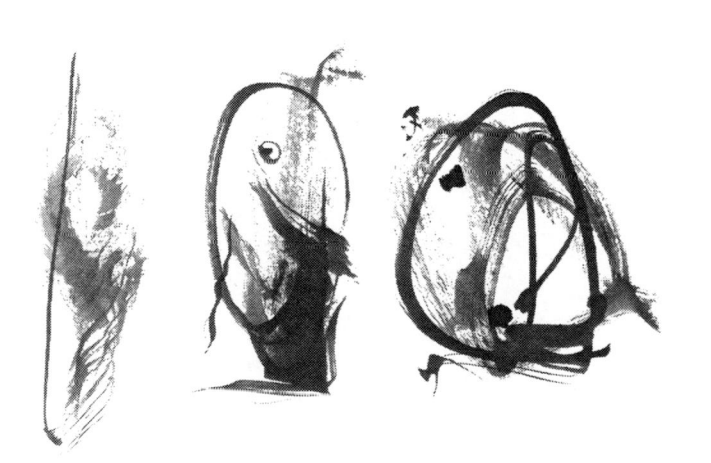

Do not worry
for the body or for the beings
in this world. First, recognise yourself
as the unchanging Awareness in
which all appears, and all else will
be seen to be taken care of.

If only you would give up
the idea that you are the body
and stay as Awareness only,
your mind would come naturally
to silence and peace.

Here are a few more *beliefs*
worth discarding:

If 'it' is meant to happen, 'it' will happen.

The Self is not an event.
It is ever present.

'I am not ready.'

The Self is already
what you are: Timeless.

Spiritual practice or study leads to enlightenment.

Find out who is doing all these
and what is aware of this doer. Then be That.

I am unable to concentrate.

You are That which is
aware of concentration and
lack of concentration.

Contemplate That!

Better
to see that mind
is nothing
but the imagination
of the Self.

All
phenomenal activity is
observed inside
my unmoving Being.

I am wordless Reality.
I am the eternal silence,
the space in space
and the light
of existence.

Beloved,

To let someone else solve your
problems may appear far easier
than solving them yourself.
The ego-mind is lazy
towards discovering Truth.

We already know that another
cannot experience nor
mature on one's behalf. Knowledge
and experience can only be
called true when it is confirmed
inside your own heart.

If you merely utter or repeat
what others say, you are no wiser
than a parrot.

Awakening
is to recognise clearly
That
which is already perfect
within yourself.

You, being your Self,
unknowingly inspire others
to be themselves.
This is true sharing.

❧

Learn to watch
the play of personal emotions,
habit and conditioning
while remaining as the silent
and invisible Witness.
This is the way of all
who have secured lasting freedom.
Be one of them!

❧

An experience is a relationship
between a phenomenal 'I'-entity
and the object of interest or attention
with which it is engaged.

The experience of the Self is an exception,
for the Self experiences non-dual,
non-phenomenal recognition
of its own indivisible reality.
This is a mystery unravelled only
through direct experience.

Love
does not need to be
a love story.

We become entangled
in the mind stream, because we
allow perishable things
to become more important
than our Being.

'Keep quiet' means
stop pursuing thoughts.

Even knowledge
came after you, because
it is you who know
knowledge and ignorance.
Who can you be?

Don't be hasty.
Contemplate this!

Can the knower
of knowledge be known?
And if so, by whom?

Let your eyes remain empty
of interpretation and
the seeing will occur in silence.
Attention craves to go out shopping
through the senses.
Leave the senses to function naturally
while keeping attention
merged in the heart.
Observe the omnipresence
of pure Awareness.

Don't define the Self,
Be the Self.

Water does not
know it is wet. Fire has no
knowledge of heat.

A road does not know
it goes anywhere.
A mountain does not
know it is still.

Distance is not aware
of measurement. Space is not
aware it is infinite.

Time does not know
it is passing. The sky does
not know it is above.

Then, who or what knows anything?
And what knows that?

The 'I'
is the final garment
to be cast off. It is the bikini
of the Being.

Now that you have learnt
what cannot be taught,
go your way.

Now that you have seen
what cannot be shown,
go your way.

Now that you have discovered
that which was not hidden,
go your way.

Now that we are united in
what is inseparable,
go your way.

Now that you have returned to
where you have never left,
go your way.

Now that you know That
which has no path,

go your own way.

Ego needs past. Ego needs future.
Ego needs identity
—Beingness does not,
so impressions don't register
or linger.
If they do, it is not due
to individuality but because
the cosmos
is appearing like that.
The sense of individuality
is also an expression of Consciousness.
It is also Consciousness,
but it is a crude form of Consciousness.
Ego is also Self.
Jiva is Shiva.
But it is Shiva with a complex.

❧

'I Am' is unbound Being.

❧

First, know you are already free.
This is the unique recognition, insight
and fruit born of self-inquiry;
to reveal our inherent freedom as eternal being.
Thereafter, practice is only to fend off the tendency
to doubt this freedom.

The sadhu
is the happy child of God.
He has no worries,
having left the cares of the world behind.
Sitting joyfully on the lap of God,
he abides in undisturbed peace,
effortlessly immersed in the Supreme.

May all beings awaken swiftly
to the single Truth
from which all emanate.
May all be happy in the knowing
that we are one family of being
with one common heart,
a Heart of imageless perfection.

Making a fortress
out of non-dual Truth
is the ultimate
escape and defence
for the ego
parading as the Self.

GLOSSARY

Ananda	Bliss of the Self
Brahman	Absolute non-dual Reality. The Supreme Being beyond the comprehension of the mind
Dharma	Truth in action; natural religion of being; that which upholds order and harmony in the universe
Dharma eye	Discernment of Truth
Eureka!	'I've found it!' Utterance attributed to the ancient Greek mathematician Archimedes
Japa	Repetition of a sacred word, mantra or the name of God
Jiva	Individual soul or ego
Prasad	Blessed offerings partaken by devotees, after being first offered to God
Sadhu	Ascetic, wandering monk
Shiva	Highest God, Pure Consciousness
Sarcophagus	Stone coffin, commonly associated with Egyptian mummies
Satguru	A spiritual preceptor of the highest attainment, one who has realised the ultimate Truth. Also the inner Guru, one's true Self, the impersonal Absolute
Satsang	Association with the highest Truth

MOOJI
(ANTHONY PAUL MOO-YOUNG)

Advaita zen master Mooji is unlike anyone else you are likely to meet, for he compels one to question one's very nature and existence. From the very first encounter, people from all walks of life are deeply touched by his indefinable presence, and perhaps for the very first time experience a natural sense of happiness and peace as they come to discover who or what they truly are.

Born in Jamaica, Mooji moved to London, UK, as a teenager. In 1987, an encounter with a Christian mystic inspired Mooji to 'walk out of his life'—an expression he uses to convey the profundity of that meeting. In 1993, Mooji travelled to India, where seemingly by chance, he met his Master Sri HWL Poonja, or 'Papaji', as he is affectionately known by his devotees. At Papaji's feet, whatever still remained of an active ego was finally uprooted.

Recognising Mooji's radiance, people from various parts of the world soon began to approach him to simply sit in his presence and to ask questions regarding their search for Truth. The capacity to guide them arose spontaneously in him. Although his presence exudes a compassionate and devotional fragrance, his uncompromising love for Truth is also potently communicated through his method of self-inquiry. It is an unsparing light which quickly dispels the delusions and suffering common to human experiencing. In his direct and open interactions, each one who meets Mooji with a genuine urge for freedom is pulled by his profound unconditional love and the power of his pointings into the recognition of the infinite Self we already are.

Mooji presently resides at Monte Sahaja in Portugal where he continues to share satsang with all those who come with a sincere desire for discovering the Truth.

ACKNOWLEDGEMENTS

From the Publisher

Our deepest gratitude goes out to Robert Larson of Bokförlaget Robert Larson AB, Johanneshov, Sweden, and Julian Noyce of Non-Duality Press, Salisbury, England, whose encouragement allowed the seed to sprout into Mooji Media. Julian's selfless guidance and sharing of his experience in particular helped this imprint come to fruition.

From the Author and Editors

Mooji, Zenji and Manjusri express their deepest love and acknowledge all those who participated in the compilation of this book. These include: Radha, Mirabai (Martha Callejas), Omkara, Nataraaj (Noé J. Peyre) and Tara P. Paldo, who over the years gleaned quotes during open satsangs and in private; Jyoti for the wonderful book cover design; Julien Aigret, Nirvana, Sankari Marinelli, Marco Brito, Tara, Nataraaj, Jyoti and Jaya Deva, whose photography captures such intimacy and beauty; Shree and Priya for their steady and efficient administrative support; and the team of Turiya, Arun, Nataraaj and Muni with whom we spent many days and nights selecting quotes, scanning, retouching drawings and typesetting.

Who can put into words the joy and dynamic grace which transpire when a group of people come together on a project of Love? We thank you all for your unique contribution, patience, time and energy, enthusiasm, laughter and most of all, your heart-infused presence.

With Love. Om Shanti.

❧

Go where you want.
Move as you will.
Do whatever your heart desires,
only don't identify.
Don't say,
'This is who or what I am.'

❧

Further details about Mooji's
work and schedule
are available on the website
www.mooji.org

For information about Mooji's
other books, *White Fire,*
Before I Am, and *Breath of the Absolute,*
and satsang recordings
in audio and video formats,
you are welcome to visit
www.mooji.org/shop

Video and audio satsangs
can also be found on
www.mooji.tv

Mooji is also on Facebook
www.facebook.com/moojiji

For additional information and
enquiries please contact:

Mooji Media Publications

office@moojimedia.com

www.moojimedia.com

*Surely,
the 'I am the body' belief
is the root cause
of all evil in this world.*

White Fire
Spiritual insights and teachings of
advaita zen master Mooji

Published by
Mooji Media Publications (2014)

Colour Edition (Paperback)
384 pages
ISBN 978-1908408181
Available from
www.mooji.org/shop

Standard Edition (Paperback)
384 pages
ISBN 978-1908408198
Available from Amazon

White Fire is a collection of close to 800 sayings which encapsulate and compress Mooji's essential spiritual teachings into pill form. These end-of-the-road pointings, when swallowed, are like divine grenades that wipe out suffering and delusion thus revealing one's true nature as perfect and timeless being.

"Fire burns everything leaving only ashes.
But there is a fire so fierce it burns even ashes —White Fire.
Burn me like this, O White Fire, Grace of God,
until nothing remains but You." —Mooji

Although *White Fire* is full of wise, direct and encouraging guidance, it is not for the faint-hearted seeker who is only looking to reinforce a spiritual identity or projections. For those who come with openness and a Yes in their heart for Truth, may the white fire in this book ignite within your heart, leaving only the clear space of pure seeing and being.

Before I Am: Second Edition
The Direct Recognition of Truth

Published by
Mooji Media Publications (2012)

272 pages
Paperback ISBN 978-1908408136
Ebook ISBN 978-1908408167

Available from
www.mooji.org/shop

Before I Am is a selection of dialogues between Mooji, a warm-hearted spiritual master, and seekers of peace, truth and freedom. This second edition expands upon the first with 100 pages of previously unpublished dialogues, fresh quotes, brush drawings and photographs.

While Mooji's presence carries a devotional fragrance, the words and drawings that spring from his Being are of the nature of non-duality. At times humorous, at times tender, occasionally sharp and always loving, Mooji responds to questioners as they speak of fear, suffering, confusion, relationships, spiritual practice and how to live their lives in peace. Yet it is Mooji's unsparing pointing to Truth, through the method of self-inquiry, which forms the essence of this book. His words represent unwavering invitations to investigate the nature of the Self and to rest effortlessly as the fullness and emptiness of Beingness. His answers encourage, challenge and never fail to illuminate.

Enriched with Mooji's exquisite brush drawings - which add depth and a power of their own - this book is even more potent than the first. This edition acts like an unsparing sword that chops the mind and leaves you fully naked as your Self.

Breath of the Absolute
Dialogues with Mooji
The Manifest and
Unmanifest Are One

Published by
Yogi Impressions Books (2010)

228 pages (Paperback and ebook)
Paperback ISBN 978-8188479610

Paperback available from
www.mooji.org/shop

Ebook available from Amazon

Breath of the Absolute is a collection of dialogues between Mooji and sincere seekers of Truth in which he invites you to take a fresh look at yourself. Of all the subjects debated within the scope of human interest, the one undisputed fact is that we exist. What is not questioned is: As what do we exist? In these dialogues, Mooji will push your mind beyond conceptual bickering into the pulsating clarity of the Unthinkable.

"The words in this book, emanating from Silence, are an act of living grace. When Consciousness speaks, that which speaks and that which listens are One. There's no seeker, no beloved. Only... Pure Awareness flowing as Love."   —Pamela Bloom, Author of *The Power of Compassion*

"The two people in whom I have most experienced the presence of what we call the Divine are His Holiness the Dalai Lama and Mooji."
—Isabel Losada, Broadcaster and Internationally Bestselling
Author of *The Battersea Park Road to Enlightenment*

"You wake up each day from the dream; but to be free, you must also wake up from the waking state."   —Mooji